Sentinel

A collection of poems by

BUKKIE ALLISON

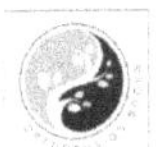

SOPHOS
SB
BOOKS

Sentinel

Copyright © 2022 by Bukkie Allison

Published by

Sophos Books

Croydon

United Kingdom

In collaboration with

Credo Fusion

Lagos, Nigeria

ISBN 978-1-905669-94-3

Book cover design by *Bukkie Allison*.

Printed in the United Kingdom.

Contents

*This book is dedicated to my niece, Mosope,
and my nephews, Olamide, Alexander,
Tobias and Damilare-Ife.*

Appreciation

I have always written poems but never have I ever presented a spoken word piece until 2022 with the support of my pastor, Tayo Ladejo, Senior Pastor at my local assembly, *The Governing Church*, Lagos, Nigeria. My gratitude goes to him for his leadership and mentorship. The poems in this selection, except for SENTINEL, were written at his request and presented at our Night of Worship and Prophecy events held in 2022.

It is my prayer that as you read (and meditate upon) each poem, Holy Spirit will inscribe upon your heart the message of God's love with the same force with which each piece was created.

Selah

Prologue

I still remember every single moment of writing the poem, *This Vessel is Empty*. It was electric. I started first to read the account of the potter in the book of Jeremiah chapter 18. And then suddenly, the words started to bubble up inside of me. It felt like my belly was a den of words that had caught fire, and the words of the poem started to locate themselves and align themselves together.

I literarily felt the words seep through my pen (in this case, my fingers) as I typed on my phone. I felt mild tremors of His stirring within me, as each stanza pushed its way through forcefully with fluidity. There was no blockage, only flow. It was the most beautiful experience. How Holy Spirit writes through us and in us, scribbling the heart of Father God with a desperate affection that is nothing other than His everlasting love.

It is my prayer that as you read (and meditate upon) each poem, the Holy Spirit will inscribe upon your heart the message of God's love with the same force with which each piece was created.

Selah

This

Vessel

is

Empty

This vessel is empty
Not as the world terms empty vessels
Good for nothings
Show-offs
Still,
This vessel is empty
Empty as God requires it
Good for service
Empty but with essence

This vessel is empty
It's hollow belly crying out to be filled
It's clay body longing to be touched
To be filled with oil
And touched by fire

This vessel is empty
Empty of profanities and idle babbling
Empty of ungodliness and heresies
This vessel is empty
Not as the world scorns emptiness
Calling them out as noise makers
Saying empty vessels are the loudest
This vessel is empty
Empty as God requires
Calling them together as vessels unto honour

Vessels of clay moulded in the light of the morning

This vessel is empty
It's hollow interior shaped with care and with intention
With the loving hands of the Potter in secret
For the sole purpose of being filled with water and with oil
In order to fill empty vessels with oil and with water
That in being emptied it shall be filled to be emptied again

This vessel is empty
It's clay exterior caked with fire
The marks of the Potter engraved with desire
Are seen in lines and curves and circles and spirals and lines and curves and circles and spirals
Around this clay exterior we see the marks of the Master
Lines of His story and circles of His journey

This vessel is empty
Empty and waiting
Waiting and pinning
For His oil and His water and His fire
Waiting to be filled in order to be emptied
again

Anchor in the Storm

Allow me to tell you a story
About a young man who knew how to
strum the strings of my heart
As a young boy he was foretold to be king
And his brothers, in envy, will treat him as
alien instead of kin
In the heat of the sun
When he watched over sheep
just like I watched over him
I taught him to vent his anger on the wolf
the lion and the bear
David weathered many storms
Many times they could have swallowed him
alive
But through each high wave and thunder
Together we meandered through dark caves
and scorching deserts

Allow me to tell you a story
About a tough, bitter, stone-hearted man
Saul was on a mission to stir up trouble
But alas I had other plans
After we were introduced
His life soon was riddled with trouble
Like a stray can riddled with bullets
Many expected Paul to crumble

Under the pressure
But beneath that pressure
There I was holding him up
Through shipwrecks and mob attacks
Through prison breaks and public
humiliation
Beaten
Wounded
Deserted
Forgotten
Falsely accused and
Sentenced to death
In all these I kept his head above water
Disallowing the torrents to keep him under

Allow me to tell you a story
About a rogue prophet called Jonah
When he shunned my Father's will
Regarding Nineveh
And found himself on board a ship going
nowhere
I whispered and the waters awoke
They swooshed high and came tumbling
down again
Right and left
The ship was tossed n flung

Dancing on the precipice of destruction
When the men feared for their lives
Jonah offered to give his life for theirs
Just like I gave mine for his
The men lifted him overboard
And tossed him into the eye of the storm
Quickly!
I shoved a wandering whale in his direction
And commanded it to harbour Jonah for a
season

I wonder
Do you see yourselves in these men?
I could tell you about Bathsheba
Torn between two men and a baby
Or Tamar
The one that was rejected over and over
and over again by the men meant to love
her and shelter her
I could tell you about Priscilla and Aquila
Forced out of their home
By a vile political policy

I wonder
Do you see yourselves in these men and
women?

In peril
In war
In famine
In distress
and even in death

I remain Protector, Anchor, Saviour and Lord.

Magnificence

Magnificent Voice
That spoke through winds that blew from
any direction, forecasting the coming flood
on a land that has never known rain,
Foretelling the destruction of all flesh
Giving minute details of cubits, lengths,
width, height, depth and mass that formed
the benevolent Ark that man made

Magnificent Mind
That called them in twos, pairing mate with
mate, male to female, guiding feet of fours
and six and twos and eights
Calling together the species that God made
into the benevolent Ark that man made

Magnificent Breath
That blew upon the firmaments above
firmaments
And down came the showers that swelled
the waters that carried the Ark that carried
the species upon the floods that covered
the earth that God made

Magnificent Promise
That coloured the sky in a rainbow spectrum
of light that hugged the firmaments that
poured the showers that swelled the waters
that carried the Ark that carried the species
that floated upon the floods that covered
the earth that God made

Magnificent Potter
That formed from clay a being like Himself
Three in one and one in three
Having spirit, soul and body
Like Father, Son and Spirit
Breathing into moulded nostrils His
tripartite essence
That made man that made the Ark that
carried the species that floated upon the
waters and upon the floods that covered
the earth that God made

Magnificent Beginning
That called the light out of the darkness
and separated night from day,
differentiating stars, and moon and sun,
seed from seed, fruit from fruit, tree from
tree, man from woman

He housed the galaxies in the cosmos and
the seas in the firmaments above the
firmaments
That poured the showers that swelled the
waters that carried the Ark that carried the
species that floated upon the floods that
covered the earth that God made

Magnificent One
That named the beginning the beginning, He
called the end from the origins. His back is
covered with eyes and His front is robed in
light. Whoever sees His back receives sight
and he who sees His front becomes as
nought.
Yes, who has seen Him and lived?
For we came from His ending and are
returning to His beginning.
His ways are past finding out. The one who
made the showers that swelled the waters
that carried the Ark that carried the
species that floated upon the floods that
covered the earth that He made out of His
Mag-ni-fi-cent Voice

Alpha and Omega
The Mag-ni-fi-cent

Sentinel

noun
1. a solja or guard whose job is to stand and keep watch.

Stand, watchman, stand!
Watch, watchman, watch
Watchman write
Scribble your prayers into the expanse
Incubate upon the future

Fight warrior fight
War, warrior, war
Warrior write
Unsheathe your sword for your pen is your
sword

See prophet see
Prophesy, prophet, prophesy
Prophet write
Release the seed of the future
Your ink bears the seed of the future

Stand sentinel stand
Watch, sentinel, watch
Sentinel write
Stand upon the walls and look into the
distant horizon
Establish pathways into birthing rooms of
tomorrow
Midwife the mind and will of YHWH

Watch, sentinel, watch
Peer with eagles eyes into the great beyond
The future is before you oh Sentinel
Rise on your feet
Gaze upon the break of this glorious dawn
For beyond these lines of enemy embankments
Is a victory so glorious
So round so mighty
Descending the heights
Like an unrelenting snowball
Rolling with YHWHs force
To crush these ranks of enemy lines
Bringing their spoils to the foot of the wall
Upon which you stand oh sentinel

See, sentinel, See
Peer with eagle eyes into the great beyond
Travel with Me upon the wings of prophecy
Into the future of distant horizons
Where YHWH hatches victories for wars yet
untold

Watch, sentinel, Watch
War, warrior, war
Prophesy, prophet, prophesy
Write, sentinel, Write

Follow me into a white expanse
Of adventures waiting to be lived
Of fantasies waiting to be inked
Of mysteries waiting to be told

Born in a Manger

Have you seen a lowly manger?
A smelly raggedy rack for fodder
You can call it feeder
For it is used to hold food for cattle and
colts alike
It could be a teeny creeping feeder
Carrying food to wiggly lambs
Or a trailer-mounted feeder
Bearing food to brawny brute horses

Mangers ensure lamb, sheep, and horses
feed healthily
They keep the sheep nourished
Well-fed and well-bred
They are food carriers
They are nutrition bearers
Can't you see?
The manger is to livestock
What a mother is to a suckling babe

Little wonder
The saviour of the world
Chose to be born in a lowly manger
Feed My Lamb, feed My sheep
If you love Me, feed My sheep
Give them bread

Give them wine
Give them fish baked in the red flames of
My passion

While shepherds watched their flock by
night
Down in a manger
Fodder was swapped with Light
His body is bread
And the blood that was spilled is wine
Never again will His lamb go hungry
Never will His sheep want for bread
For the Good Shepherd was born in a manger
Bread of Life asleep in a raggedy trough
Emmanuel, He is God with us
The Shepherd who laid down His life for His
sheep

Other Books by Bukkie

Qoheleth

A Prayer for You

Chasing the Silence

5 Ways to Protect the Anointing

5 Ways to Steward the Anointing

Contact the Author

email
therivercourse@gmail.com

instagram
@the_rivercourse

facebook
www.facebook.com/bukkie.allison

Bukkie Allison is a scribe dedicated to seeking out treasures in God's word and sharing them with believers around the world, for edification of the body until we all grow into maturity in Christ. She finds great joy in sharing her solemn journeys in God with others. Apart from writing instructional teachings, Bukkie is passionate about unearthing untold life affirming stories and publishing them for posterity. She lives in Lagos, Nigeria, where she works as chief strategy officer for her indie publishing company.